What Is the Story of Smokey Bear?

T0201589

by Steve Korté

illustrated by Robert Squier

Penguin Workshop

For George and Gilbert—SK

For Forest Ranger James E. Taylor's great-grandchildren, Stanley, Phoebe, and Ione—RS

PENGUIN WORKSHOP
An imprint of Penguin Random House LLC, New York

First published in the United States of America by Penguin Workshop,
an imprint of Penguin Random House LLC, New York, 2024

The name and character of Smokey Bear are the property of the United States,
as provided by 16 U.S.C. 580p-1, and are used with the permission
of the Forest Service, U.S. Department of Agriculture.

PENGUIN is a registered trademark and PENGUIN WORKSHOP is a trademark
of Penguin Books Ltd. WHO HQ & Design is a registered trademark
of Penguin Random House LLC.

Visit us online at penguinrandomhouse.com.

Library of Congress Cataloging-in-Publication Data is available.

Printed in the United States of America

ISBN 9780593385708 (paperback)   10 9 8 7 6 5 4 3 2 1 CJKW
ISBN 9780593385975 (library binding)   10 9 8 7 6 5 4 3 2 1 CJKW

Contents

What Is the Story of Smokey Bear?

Television became popular around the world in the early 1950s. In those days, television screens were much smaller than they are today—some were only fifteen inches wide—and shows were broadcast in black and white. Families would gather close to the small screen to watch their favorite programs. In the evening, there were news broadcasts, dramas, comedies, and music shows. Saturday morning was the time for children's shows. Kids would wake up early and huddle near the TV, often still in their pajamas, to enjoy the adventures of their favorite animated cartoon characters. And in between the cartoons there were lots of commercials promoting toys, cereal, candy, and all sorts of fun stuff that kids desired.

It was during the early 1950s that a famous bear from the forest made his debut in a television commercial. He was already well known from posters and radio ads. But a series of TV ads gave the public a chance to see him in action for the first time.

One of his early commercials opened with an animated view of a forest. A little boy was shown enjoying a picnic in an open space with some wildlife pals, including a bird, a deer, and a squirrel. As the boy walked through the forest, he gazed at livestock grazing in a field, timber being harvested, and a beautiful waterfall.

"A forest is sure a lot of things!" the boy exclaimed happily.

Suddenly, a flame erupted in the forest.

The deep voice of a narrator warned, "Yes, but let a little fire get started, catch on, destroy, and your forest is nothing!"

Soon, the forest was reduced to smoldering stumps of burned trees.

Just then, a tall bear appeared next to the boy. The bear was wearing jeans and a forest ranger's hat.

"You have so many reasons to protect your forest," said the bear. "Remember, only *you* can prevent forest fires!"

The name of the bear was Smokey. He was already a beloved fictional character. And soon he would become the face of fire prevention all around the world.

CHAPTER 1
Disappearing Forests

When the English colonists arrived on the East Coast of North America in 1607, more than a billion acres of forest stretched across the country. It has been estimated that there were about six million Native Americans living in the country at the time. For centuries the Native communities had successfully managed the land. They were careful to maintain the number of forests while still finding enough space for their homes and crops. The newly arrived colonists, though, did not hesitate to cut down trees to make room for crops. They also used the fallen wood for housing, fences, and fuel. As more and more new colonists arrived, the forests started to shrink.

Newly planted seeds could not grow trees fast enough to meet the increasing demand for wood.

"By 1800, a wood shortage developed near large East Coast cities," said the historian Terry West.

"By the 1830s, so many trees had been razed
[cut down] that commercial lumbering began
shifting to the Great Lakes region of Michigan,
Wisconsin and Minnesota."

After the forests in those states were wiped out, the lumber industry shifted to forests in the South and along the Pacific coast. By 1918, as the

country's population grew to 108 million people, it's estimated a total of 260 million acres of forest land in North America had vanished!

Two Fires in 1871

On October 8, 1871, a fire broke out in Chicago, Illinois. It started in a barn on the southwest side of town but quickly expanded and swept through the city. Three hundred people died in the fire, and one-third of the city's population lost their homes.

The Great Chicago Fire

The blaze was so deadly that it came to be known as the Great Chicago Fire.

On that same day, another fire started in a forest in Wisconsin that was roughly two hundred miles north of Chicago. Known as the Peshtigo Fire, it also grew quickly and roared through rural areas of Wisconsin and Michigan. It is believed that more than 1,200 people died in that fire, and over a million acres of land were scorched. The Peshtigo Fire was the deadliest fire in the history of the United States.

Were the two blazes connected? No one knows for sure, but some people believe a falling meteor may have caused one or both fires.

All during this period, the number of forest fires in America increased as European settlers moved west across the country. Some people even set forest fires for *fun* during the nineteenth century! Even though it's hard to believe, there was a contest during the 1800s to see who could set the biggest forest fire in the Cascade mountain range in western North America.

Unfortunately, most Americans ignored the dangers of forest fires. They just assumed that there would always be enough trees for everyone.

CHAPTER 2
Wartime Worries

In the early 1900s, a government agency called the United States Forest Service was established to protect America's woodlands and watch over a growing number of government-managed national forests. The Forest Service also tried to educate the public on the dangers of forest fires. But it wasn't until the 1940s, during World War II, that the American public really started to focus on the idea of forest fire prevention.

World War II began in 1939, when Britain declared war on Germany because Germany sent soldiers to invade Poland. It lasted until 1945 and involved major countries from around the world. Although most of the early days of the war were fought in Europe, there were also attacks made by the Japanese military on United States soil. The most famous of those attacks was the bombing of Pearl Harbor in Hawaii on December 7, 1941.

The bombing of Pearl Harbor

The United States Forest Service

During the 1870s, the United States government started taking charge of some of the forests and wilderness areas in America. This was a new idea and led to the creation of government-managed forests, such as Yellowstone Park Timberland Reserve, which is now part of the Shoshone and Bridger-Teton National Forests in Wyoming. The United States Senate and House of Representatives, the two branches of the government responsible for making laws, decided in 1881 to create a new Division of Forestry. Its mission was to manage forests, plant trees, and educate the public on forest preservation.

By 1905, 63 million acres of woodlands in the United States were being managed by the government. That same year, the agency became known as the USDA (United States Department of

Agriculture) Forest Service. Over the following years, more woodlands came under the supervision of the government. Today, there are nearly thirty thousand Forest Service employees. The Forest Service manages 193 million acres of land, which is an area roughly the size of Texas.

More than two thousand people were killed at Pearl Harbor, and a thousand others were injured. This was the main reason why America joined the war against Japan, Germany, and Italy. These three countries came to be known as the Axis powers during this war.

In February 1942, a Japanese submarine surfaced off the coast of Southern California and fired explosive shells at an oil field near the town of Santa Barbara. The oil field was not far from the Los Padres National Forest. Fortunately, there were no injuries and very little damage. Throughout the war, more than nine thousand Japanese explosive fire balloons were launched at the western United States.

Explosive fire balloon

San Bernardino National Forest

There are four national forests in Southern California, and many people worried that the Axis powers might try to start a large-scale forest fire that could spread to nearby towns. All across the country, there was a real fear that America's enemies could start fires and then invade the country, causing loss of life and destruction of personal and state-owned property.

During the war, the Forest Service teamed up with two organizations, the War Advertising Council and the National Association of State Foresters. Together they created the Cooperative Forest Fire Prevention Program (CFFP) and developed a "Wartime Forest Fire Prevention" advertising campaign. The goal of the ad campaign was to raise public awareness of the dangers of forest fires and how those fires might harm the war effort.

In 1942, they created a frightening poster showing a smiling enemy soldier holding a flaming match. The caption on the poster read, "Careless matches aid the Axis. Prevent Forest Fires." Other posters were created, showing scary pictures of Germany's chancellor Adolf Hitler and Japan's prime minister Hideki Tojo surrounded by flames. Below them was this message: "Our Carelessness—Their Secret Weapon. Prevent Forest Fires."

Thirty-six million copies of these fire prevention materials were sent to schools and government agencies around the country. But the response from the public was not what the Forest Service had expected. It turned out that the posters were *too* scary!

"There was a lot of debate about the posters the first few years," admitted Jim Felton, who worked on the ad campaign. "They weren't well received and the schools didn't want to put them up."

So in 1943, the CFFP program decided to create a new ad campaign that was less scary to spread the message. But they needed someone to star in the ads. Who would the public embrace as the face of forest fire prevention?

FOREST FIRE PREVENTION MASCOT IDEAS

CHAPTER 3
Search for a Mascot

The group started working on new ads and posters to teach the public about the need to protect forests and the dangers of forest fires. They decided that an animal might be a good choice to star in the ads, and so they reached out to one of the world's most popular movie studios—Walt Disney.

Walt Disney

A few years earlier, the Walt Disney movie studio had produced the successful animated movies *Snow White and the Seven Dwarfs* and *Pinocchio*. In 1942, the studio released *Bambi*, the story of a young deer. Part of the movie showed Bambi's terrifying escape from a raging forest fire, so the popular deer seemed like a logical choice for the new ad campaign.

In 1944, the Disney studio agreed to loan the character Bambi to the CFFP for one year and created a large, colorful poster. It showed Bambi along with his woodland friends Thumper the rabbit and Flower the skunk. "Please, Mister, don't be careless," appeared at the top of the poster,

and at the bottom it read, "Prevent Forest Fires. Greater danger than ever!"

There were seven other fire prevention posters released that year, but the Bambi poster was the clear favorite with the public. Thousands of copies went on display at gas stations and stores across the country. Libraries in California requested eighty thousand bookmarks that featured Bambi's fire prevention message. Schoolchildren loved the Bambi poster and asked if they could bring copies of it home.

But the Bambi character was still owned by the Disney studio, and for legal reasons Bambi was only allowed to appear on that one poster.

So the ad group started thinking about a new, original character that the program could own.

Bill Bergoffen

In 1944, a man named Bill Bergoffen joined the creative team that was creating fire prevention ads and posters for the CFFP.

"We learned very quickly that animals were effective in getting people—especially the young—to react," Bergoffen said. "That was especially important because we thought we wanted to try to educate the youngsters. . . . It was the adults who started a lot of roadside woods and brush fires—they just tossed lighted matches and cigarettes away. But we thought—or hoped—children could influence their adults."

Artist Harry Rossoll, who worked on the new ad campaign, proposed a fictional Forest Service ranger character named Ranger Jim to replace Bambi. Forest Service rangers are people who work in state and national forests, managing them and helping to prevent wildfires.

Harry Rossoll

The team decided against Ranger Jim and went back to the idea of another animal mascot. Someone suggested a squirrel, but that was rejected. Next, they tried a flat-tailed beaver.

"This beaver could put out fires," recalled Rossoll. "He could flap them out with his tail. Flap, flap, flap, flap, flap."

But the team thought that it would get boring watching the beaver just flapping out fires all the time.

Finally, it was decided that a large animal was the best choice, and someone suggested a bear. A bear was the most powerful animal in the forest.

Also, a bear could stand upright on its rear legs and even look like it was strong enough to put out a fire.

Once they made the decision to go with a bear, all that was left to do was to design and name it.

CHAPTER 4
Smokey Is Born

There were many people involved in the creation of America's number one wildfire preventing bear. People from the Forest Service, the National Association of State Foresters, the War Advertising Council, and an outside advertising company all pitched ideas for the new bear mascot.

On August 9, 1944, program director Richard Hammett sent out a letter suggesting the look and mission of the new character:

- "Nose short (Panda type), color black or brown; expression appealing, knowledgeable, quizzical, perhaps wearing a campaign (or Boy Scout) hat that typifies the outdoors and the woods

- "A bear that walks on his hind legs; that can be shown putting out a warming fire with a bucket of water; dropping by parachute to a fire; reporting a fire by phone from a lookout; plowing a fire-line around a new-made clearing; building a campfire in the right place and way; carrying a rifle like G. I. Joe, etc.

- "Message: 'PREVENT FOREST FIRES'"

Artist Albert Staehle was chosen to draw this new character. His drawing of a bear arrived in the Forest Service headquarters in September. It showed a bear pouring a bucket of water to drown a campfire. The bear was not wearing any clothes.

"Staehle had drawn a bare bear," said Bill

Albert Staehle

Bergoffen, who admitted that a few people expressed concerns about the idea of a naked bear as the mascot.

Bergoffen suggested that the bear should wear

"dungarees," which was another word for blue jeans.

A team member named Fred Schoder suggested that the bear should wear a ranger's hat. Everyone agreed that a ranger's hat would make the bear look more official.

Finally, the bear needed a name. Stories vary on how he ended up being called "Smokey Bear." Some say that the name was suggested by Richard Hammett, who was working on the ad campaign. Others say the name was inspired by "Smokey Joe" Martin, a famous former member of New York City's fire department.

Once he had been named Smokey, the bare bear drawing was returned to Albert Staehle with instructions to dress him in blue jeans and add a ranger's hat. Staehle quickly delivered a revised drawing. Now Smokey was wearing clothes as he put out a campfire.

For the final touch, a caption was placed below the drawing that read, "Smokey says—Care *will* prevent 9 out of 10 forest fires!"

The image was quickly printed on posters, bookmarks, and covers that children could wrap around their schoolbooks.

"Smokey Joe" Martin (1862–1941)

Joseph B. Martin worked as a firefighter in New York City for more than forty-six years. He became a fireman in 1884 and, after several promotions, became assistant chief of the New York City Fire Department in 1919. His firefighting skills were legendary. One time, while battling a blaze in 1898, he kicked open the door of a smoke-filled room on the fourth floor of a building. Suddenly, the floor collapsed! Martin fell through the third, second, and first floors, all the while surrounded by flaming debris. Finally, he collapsed in the basement. He was taken to a hospital, where everyone thought he was sure to die. But in the middle of the night, he startled everyone by yelling for a glass of water. Three months later, he walked out of the hospital and resumed his firefighting career. He continued to respond to fire alarms until his death in 1941.

Just as World War II was ending in 1945, Smokey Bear was introduced to America. The new posters and other items were mailed to

schools and public libraries all over the country. Now they just had to wait to see how the public would react to the fire prevention bear.

Smokey's Birthday

There is some debate about Smokey Bear's birthdate. The first public record about creating a Smokey Bear character is dated August 9, 1944. That's the date Richard Hammett sent his letter with the first details about the wildfire preventing bear. But Smokey Bear didn't appear on a poster until the spring of 1945, which was eight months later. However, starting in 1954, the Forest

Service officially recognized Smokey's birthdate as August 9, 1944. Posters celebrating Smokey's birthday have been produced over the years, and each year Smokey receives birthday cards from his admirers. In 2022, there was a live streamed online party for Smokey's seventy-eighth birthday.

CHAPTER 5
Becoming a Star

Smokey Bear made his first public appearance on a poster in 1945, and he quickly became a celebrity.

"Almost overnight Smokey became a popular character, especially in contrast to other materials the campaign had used," said Bill Bergoffen.

"Letters started pouring in from kids, and we got a strong, positive media reaction. Suddenly we had a large demand for Smokey Bear materials."

Dear Smokey, We Love You! From, Nancy

Smokey's image and his message about preventing forest fires started appearing in hundreds of magazines and newspapers. Children recognized Smokey just about as much as they recognized Santa Claus! Kids would write letters and just put "Smokey Bear" on the envelope, and the US Postal Service knew to forward the letters to the Forest Service offices in Washington, DC.

Zip Code 20252

Over the years, so many children wrote letters to Smokey Bear that in 1964 the Post Office gave Smokey his own zip code: 20252. He is the only fictional character in the United States to receive a zip code.

Here is his full address:

Smokey Bear

Washington, DC 20252

It has been estimated that in the years leading up to 1964, Smokey received more mail than anyone in Washington, DC, including the president of the United States. In some years, Smokey received over 200,000 letters and postcards.

In 1946, it was decided that Smokey needed a voice. This was in the days before TV sets became widely available, and people listened to radios for news and entertainment.

Jackson Weaver

A man named Jackson Weaver, who worked for a radio station in Washington, DC, auditioned and was chosen as the voice of Smokey Bear. Smokey's most famous spoken phrase made its first appearance in a 1947 radio commercial: "Remember, only *you* can prevent forest fires."

To get just the right deep sound with a little bit of echo for the bear's message, Bergoffen asked Weaver to put his head into a bucket when they first recorded Smokey's voice. After a while, Weaver learned how to make the same deep sounds without the use of a bucket!

Smokey's Five Rules

Over the years, Smokey's message about fire prevention has expanded to these five easy-to-remember rules:

1. Only you can prevent wildfires.

2. Always be careful with fire.

3. Never play with matches or lighters.

4. Always watch your campfire.

5. Make sure your campfire is completely out before leaving it.

As a public service, radio stations played Smokey's commercials for free. By 1950, thanks to Smokey Bear and the talented people who created Smokey's campaign, the American public was more informed about the need to prevent forest fires than ever before. Best of all, within a few years of Smokey's introduction, the number of forest fires in the United States decreased! Experts had predicted that there would be 300,000 human-caused fires per year by 1950. Instead, the number of those fires from 1946 to 1950 was only 190,000 per year. That meant there were twenty thousand fewer human-caused fires per year in Smokey's first years.

CHAPTER 6
The Real Deal

On May 4, 1950, a fire broke out high in the Capitan Mountains of New Mexico in the United States. No one knew how it started. Perhaps it

was a careless person who threw a lit match on the ground. Or maybe a cookstove began throwing sparks when no one was paying attention. On that day, winds swept the fire through the woods, and the blaze quickly grew out of control.

Forest rangers, firefighters, Army soldiers, and Native Americans from Taos Pueblo in New Mexico battled the deadly flames for six days.

Smoke from the fire could be seen one hundred miles away. Terrified animals tried to outrun the blaze, but many died in the fire.

Some of the firefighters reported seeing a young bear cub—weighing about five pounds and probably only three months old—wandering in the burning woods. It had probably gotten separated from its mother. They decided to leave the cub alone, just in case its mother came back.

"Mother bears will go off and prowl around, maybe hunt for food, but usually come back," said Ray Bell, who worked as a game warden in New Mexico. *Game* refers to any animal that is hunted for food or sport, and it usually applies to mammals and birds. It was Bell's job as a game warden to protect wildlife in the area, manage their populations, and enforce game laws.

Ray Bell

On May 9, a group of firefighters saw the cub again.

"We found a tiny bear cub weighing about five pounds, his hair singed, and feet severely burned, clinging to a small tree at the edge of the fire chewing on the bark, apparently trying to get some food and moisture," reported another game

warden named Elliott Barker. "As we walked up the little fellow stared down at us with a bewildered look in his beady little eyes, too young to fear man but in a very unhappy predicament, apparently having lost his mother in the fire and wanting to go back to her."

One of the men reached up to grab the cub and cradled it in his arms. The firefighters decided to bring the wounded animal back to their camp.

 There they fed it condensed milk and grape jelly. Unfortunately, the food made the cub sick, and there was little that the firefighters could do to heal his burned paws and legs.

Ray Bell decided that he would take the cub into his care. Ray knew all about the Smokey Bear ad campaign, and he had an idea.

"Well, maybe there could be a live bear to go with that poster," he said. "You never know; maybe there's something there if we can save this cub."

It was probably about this time that people started calling the cub by the name of Smokey. That one decision would change the bear's life forever.

Ray flew the young animal to a veterinarian in Santa Fe, New Mexico, who bandaged Smokey's damaged paws and applied medicine to his burned skin. After a week, Ray brought the cub home with him.

"Dad brought home wild animals all the time, so another one was not something to get excited about," remembered Ray's son Don, who was fifteen years old when Smokey arrived at their home. Ray's five-year-old daughter, Judy, was delighted to meet the cub.

Ray's wife, Ruth, also wasn't surprised at the arrival of a baby bear. Although she was not a veterinarian, Ruth had a lot of experience nursing wounded animals back to health.

That first night, Ruth set her alarm clock to ring every two hours during the night so she could wake up to feed Smokey a mixture of dry cereal, milk, and honey. Slowly, the little cub regained his strength. He seemed to enjoy his new home and developed a close relationship with Ray's daughter and the family's cocker spaniel puppy, named Jet. Ruth kept a close eye on the cub to make sure he didn't harm Judy.

The only member of the Bell family whom

Smokey seemed to dislike was Ray. Perhaps it was because Ray was the one who had to change Smokey's bandages, a painful experience for the cub. Smokey made a point of biting Ray on the hand whenever he could. But Ray didn't seem to mind. He solved the problem by wearing very thick gloves when he was near the cub. And Ray continued to work on his idea of involving his furry houseguest in the famous Smokey Bear campaign.

One funny story that Ray loved to tell was about the time he and Smokey were guests together on a Santa Fe radio program. During the show, the cub leaned over so that he could bite one of Ray's ungloved hands. Ray admitted that the word he shouted in response to Smokey's bite was not at all appropriate for a live radio broadcast!

After one month at the Bells' home, Smokey was fully recovered. Ray asked a friend to take photos of the cub. Among the pictures were some of Smokey posing in front of an official Smokey Bear fire prevention poster. Ray thought that the Forest Service and the people behind the Smokey Bear campaign would be thrilled if the rescued cub became known as the real-life Smokey Bear. But it wasn't that simple. The Smokey Bear program had been a big success for five years. The Forest Service wasn't sure it wanted a *live* bear to become known as Smokey. After all, what would happen to the ad campaign when the real bear named

Smokey eventually died? And where would the real-life Smokey live?

In the end, though, the Forest Service accepted the idea, and it was arranged that Smokey the cub would be flown in a private plane to his new home at the National Zoo in Washington, DC.

The National Zoo

The National Zoo, in Washington, DC, was founded in 1889, making it one of the oldest zoos in the United States. Its official name is the Smithsonian's National Zoo and Conservation Biology Institute, and it has two locations, containing roughly 2,100 animals and 400 different species. Almost one quarter of the animals at the zoo are in danger of going extinct—which means they would disappear forever—in the wild. The longest-lived resident of the zoo is an Aldabra tortoise, which can live to be more than one hundred years old. By far the most popular National Zoo residents over the years have been giant pandas. Most of the giant pandas were on loan from China, but seven giant panda cubs were born at the National Zoo. For those who couldn't visit the zoo in person, there was a twenty-four-hour "Giant Panda Cam" where viewers could watch giant pandas Tian Tian, Mei Xiang, and Xiao Qi Ji climb trees, eat bamboo, and play on the grass. In 2023, the giant pandas were returned to China.

There was a big farewell party for Smokey the night before his departure. Everyone seemed to enjoy the party except for the guest of honor.

"Smokey came away from the party rather disgusted," Ray remembered. "I had put on a thicker pair of gloves, and his chewing was not having the effect it had had in the past."

After Smokey arrived at the National Zoo and was placed in his new outdoor quarters,

adults and children mobbed the zoo to see him. Smokey soon became the zoo's most popular resident. The cub didn't wear a pair of blue jeans or a ranger's hat, and he never appeared in any of the Smokey Bear posters. But he quickly became the living symbol of Smokey Bear. The public loved the cartoon Smokey Bear *and* the adorable cub named Smokey who lived at the National Zoo.

CHAPTER 7
Smokey the Celebrity

The Smokey Bear program continued to grow. New posters were created every year. The CFFP program developed a pattern of what they called "red years" and "green years" for the posters. A green year meant posters with positive images showing a green forest and a message such as "Let's keep them that way." For the following year, red posters would show a burned forest with a message about the danger of not being careful.

WHY?

remember—
only you can PREVENT FOREST FIRES!

Right after the Smokey campaign began, the program created a sixteen-page booklet called *Smokey Bear's Story of the Forest* that was sent to schools for free. It was a coloring book that included important lessons about forests and the animals that lived in woodlands. Over the years, more than twenty-four million copies were distributed to schoolchildren.

When television became popular in the 1950s, Smokey Bear started appearing in TV ads. The agency in charge of Smokey's TV commercials never used the bear cub Smokey who was living at the National Zoo. Instead, they showed an animated drawing of Smokey, and voice actor Jackson Weaver delivered Smokey's message about preventing forest fires. In one early animated TV commercial, a careless male camper was shown walking through a forest. Smokey's deep voice could be heard warning the man about the dangers of his lit match and smoldering campfire. At the end of the commercial, after the man had learned his lesson about fire prevention, an animated version of Smokey faced the viewer and gave his familiar message: "Remember, only *you* can prevent forest fires!"

Movie stars and musicians offered to join Smokey for radio and TV commercials. Among the many celebrities who volunteered their services were Louis Armstrong, John Wayne, Dolly Parton, and basketball superstar Kareem Abdul-Jabbar.

Kareem Abdul-Jabbar

Smokey's face—and his message—reached almost every family in America thanks to posters, ads in newspapers and magazines, and commercials on radio and TV.

Smokey Bear had become so important that in 1952, the United States Congress even passed the "Smokey Bear Act," a law that prevented anyone from using Smokey Bear's image without permission from the USDA Forest Service. Anyone who violated the law faced a fine of $250 or six months in prison, or both. The new law also required that all products using Smokey's name or image educate the public about fire prevention.

The Smokey Bear Act prevented companies from creating unauthorized Smokey T-shirts, candy, and other merchandise. One restaurant in California was even told to stop selling their Smokey Bear pancakes!

CHAPTER 8
Life at the Zoo

Back at the National Zoo, the real-life Smokey was still drawing big crowds, attracting four million visitors every year. Crowds lined up in tightly packed rows to see the famous bear. Smokey was more popular than the zoo's other big celebrity, a chimpanzee named Ham, who was the first great ape to fly in a rocket ship on a trip into space.

In 1962, zoo officials brought in a female companion for Smokey. Her name was Goldie, and she was an American black bear also from New Mexico. Game warden Ray Bell, who was Smokey's original foster father, was the one who delivered Goldie to the National Zoo.

Smokey and Goldie

Thinking about the bites he had received from Smokey the cub many years ago, Ray turned down the offer to go into Smokey's enclosure.

"I didn't know if he remembered me, but I remembered him, and there is a big difference between eight pounds and five hundred pounds," said Ray.

Sadly, Smokey and Goldie never had a cub together. Some thought that Smokey's severe burns from the forest fire may have prevented him from fathering a cub. So the zoo brought

Little Smokey

in another orphan bear cub from the same forest where Smokey was found. The one-year-old cub was called "Little Smokey" (or sometimes "Smokey Junior"). Once again, Ray Bell made the cross-country trip to deliver the cub to Washington, DC. Little Smokey joined the National Zoo in 1971.

Despite the arrival of Little Smokey, the adult Smokey still drew big crowds. But his popularity at the zoo fell to second place in 1972 when China donated two giant pandas to the National Zoo. Suddenly, everyone seemed more interested in the pandas. There was even some criticism that Smokey was not as entertaining as the pandas, who loved to play together in their enclosure. Smokey rarely paid attention to the visitors who lined up to see him. He mostly ignored them as he munched on his favorite foods: peanuts,

doughnuts, and honey sandwiches. Nowadays, of course, bears in zoos are fed a much more scientifically balanced—and healthy—diet!

In 1975, the adult Smokey Bear reached the age of twenty-five. That was roughly seventy years old in human years, which was the age that federal employees were required to retire from the government. In honor of his birthday, Smokey became the first bear to join the National Association of Retired Federal Employees. A

poster was created for the occasion, showing Smokey handing over his shovel and blue jeans to Little Smokey, with Smokey saying the words "Carry on, Little Smokey."

In the mid-1970s, Smokey's health started to decline. Like many senior animals, he began to walk more slowly because of arthritis, which caused pain in Smokey's joints, including in his knees and paws. He rarely stepped outside his pen to greet the people hoping to get a glimpse of the famous bear.

A group of children in Maine read about Smokey's health problems and sent him a letter.

"Hi, Smokey," it read. "How are you feeling?

I'm sorry that you have that kind of rheumatism. So we are sending you some honey so you will feel better."

Smokey Bear passed away on November 9, 1976, at the age of twenty-six. The people in Capitan, New Mexico, asked that his body be returned to his birthplace, where a Smokey Bear Museum had been built. The famous bear was buried at the newly created Smokey Bear Historical Park in Capitan.

Flowers and letters of sympathy poured in from children and adult admirers of Smokey. One pair of fans wrote, "Dear Smokey. I'm sorry that you died. I hope you are very happy in Heaven. We will all miss you and will be very careful with fires." Another person wrote, "Goodbye Beloved Smokey. You were the greatest guy who ever lived. . . . I will miss you a lot. Be happy in the great forests of Heaven."

A plaque was created for Smokey's last home,

and the simple first line of it reads, "This is the final resting place of the first living Smokey Bear."

Smokey Bear Museum

In the mid-1950s, the people in Capitan, New Mexico, started planning a state park and museum to honor their famous hometown bear. In 1955, construction plans were announced for an eighteen-by-thirty-two-foot log cabin that would become the Smokey Bear Museum. Located at 102 Smokey Bear Boulevard, the museum opened in 1961, with a costumed Smokey Bear making an appearance. The museum was filled with Smokey

merchandise and posters. It even included one of Smokey the cub's baby bottles used by Ruth Bell to feed him . . . complete with Smokey's teeth marks!

Two decades later, Capitan purchased more than an acre of land surrounding the museum and built the Smokey Bear Historical State Park. The park welcomed its first visitors in 1976.

SMOKEY

SMOKEY BEAR
Historical Park
CAPITAN, NEW MEXICO

CHAPTER 9
Smokey Becomes a Legend

As the Smokey Bear fire prevention campaign became more and more popular, there were increased demands for Smokey Bear products.

The first official product was a 1952 Smokey Bear doll, created by the Ideal Toy Company. It had a plastic head and a soft, furry body. Starting in 1953, the doll came with an application to join a volunteer club called the Junior Forest Rangers.

A Ranger Resigns

In 1960, a nine-year-old boy accidentally started a fire in Iowa that almost burned out of control. He was so embarrassed by what he had done that he mailed his treasured Junior Forest Ranger badge back to Smokey and resigned from the club.

He soon received a letter from Smokey, saying that his badge would be returned to him in three months if he didn't play with matches and was careful around fires.

The young boy followed Smokey's instructions, and his badge was returned to him along with an original Smokey Bear drawing!

Hundreds of thousands of kids applied to join the club, and in return they received a personal letter from Smokey, signed with his paw print, and an official kit of fire prevention materials. Other items sent to members over the years included Smokey's photograph, a shiny Junior Forest Ranger badge, a bookmark, and the lyrics and music for a song called "Smokey the Bear."

The "Smokey the Bear" song was the creation of the team of Steve Nelson and Jack Rollins, who had already written the hit songs "Frosty the Snowman" and "Peter Cottontail." In 1952, they decided to write a song honoring Smokey. The songwriters added the word "the" to Smokey Bear's name ("Smokey *the* Bear") because it fit the melody of their song better. They agreed to donate half of any money made by the song to the CFFP. The song's words and music were printed and sent to 450,000 classrooms in the United States.

"Smokey the Bear"

For many years after the "Smokey the Bear" song was first released, it was hard to find a kid in America who didn't know the lyrics. The five lines in the chorus of the song were especially popular with kids all across the country:

"Smokey the Bear, Smokey the Bear.
Prowlin' and a growlin' and a sniffin' the air.
He can find a fire before it starts to flame.
That's why they call him Smokey,
That was how he got his name."

Four record companies released their own unique versions of the jingle. The song even became the number-five best seller at the end of the year!

One of Smokey Bear's most important missions was to teach children about fire prevention. That's why forest rangers and Smokey started making personal visits to schools to talk about

fire safety rules. Employees would dress up in big Smokey Bear costumes to bring the character to life in classrooms. One of the challenges faced by the Smokey mascots was that their big, furry costumes could be very hot. So someone had the idea to put a small battery-operated fan inside the Smokey Bear suit!

On November 24, 1966, which was
Thanksgiving Day, Smokey Bear made his first
appearance as a balloon in the Macy's Thanksgiving
Day Parade in New York City. The fifty-nine-foot-tall

balloon was seen by an estimated forty million people on TV. The General Electric Company donated the $26,000 needed to build the parade balloon.

That same evening, a one-hour animated TV special called *Ballad of Smokey the Bear* was broadcast on NBC. The star of the show was Smokey's older brother, a newly created character called Big Bear who was voiced by the actor James Cagney. Smokey didn't actually appear much in the show, which mostly featured Smokey's brother and various woodland animals trying to find out who set a forest fire and was poisoning the water. But even with just a little bit of Smokey Bear, the show was a hit. It aired again in 1968 and 1969, reaching a combined total of more than sixty million viewers.

On September 6, 1969, Smokey starred in his own animated comedy-adventure program, *The Smokey Bear Show*, which aired every week on ABC for two years. Each show featured a fire prevention message and a message about protecting the environment.

Smokey was everywhere! By 1971, there were over 160 official Smokey Bear products available, including comic books, plastic hats, T-shirts, pajamas, books, breakfast cereal, jewelry, and bubble bath. Schoolkids could carry their meals in Smokey lunch boxes and cover their books in Smokey book covers.

Families could enjoy meals together dining with Smokey silverware and Smokey salt and pepper shakers, and then they could grab a dessert from their Smokey cookie jar. Surprisingly, there were also a few fire-related Smokey Bear items, including charcoal briquettes for a barbecue grill.

When the live Smokey died at the National Zoo in 1976, some people in the Forest Service and its ad agency wondered if the Smokey Bear ad campaign might suffer. There were a lot of worried discussions at the ad agency that handled the Smokey program. There were even some people there who thought that it might be time to find a new animal as the face of the fire prevention program!

"We reminded people that the live bear actually had retired in 1975, and we encouraged them to not lose sight of the fact that the *real* Smokey Bear was a poster," said Don Hansen, who worked on the Smokey campaign. "The living symbol was certainly the most glorious part of the story, but it offered the least about what the public needed to know. The issue was how to prevent forest fires and be safe in the woods."

"We thought of Smokey as a symbol—not a real animal," said Ann King, another person who worked on the Smokey Bear ads. "Our Smokey . . . has fingers and thumbs; he is not a real bear. Real bears are scary; Smokey Bear is gentle. Real bears don't wear Levi's and a hat."

Fortunately, Smokey Bear ended up keeping his job, and his campaign stayed as effective as ever. Smokey's face continued to appear everywhere: posters, newspapers, magazines, billboards, and TV commercials.

Starting in 1977, a firefighter and major Smokey Bear fan in Pennsylvania named Mike Marchese started a letter-writing campaign to get Smokey's image on a postage stamp.

"I wrote letters to the Postal Service, President

Carter, all the senators," remembered Mike. "I . . . wrote to everyone I could think of—movie stars, the Boy Scouts, *Good Morning America*, *Reader's Digest*. I sent sixteen letters to President Reagan. Then I went to the schools and asked kids to write letters that I could send to Congress."

Mike estimated that he mailed fifty to sixty letters a week and probably spent five to six thousand dollars on his campaign! His efforts

 finally paid off. In 1984, to celebrate Smokey's fortieth anniversary, the Postal Service issued a Smokey Bear stamp. Smokey was the first bear to receive that honor.

Over the years, sales of Smokey-related products have brought in millions of dollars. And all of those funds have been used for fire prevention education programs.

CHAPTER 10
Smokey Today

Only a handful of illustrated characters from the 1930s and 1940s are as popular today as when they were created. Among them are Superman, Batman, Wonder Woman, Captain America . . . and Smokey Bear.

And like some of those other heroes, Smokey Bear has even taken to the skies! In 1993, a group in New Mexico launched the first Smokey Bear hot air balloon. Called the Friends of Smokey Bear Balloon, it measured almost a hundred feet high and weighed about 1,100 pounds. It was so popular that reservations to fly in the balloon had to be scheduled as far as three years in advance.

In 2012, Smokey Bear even went to space. The crew of NASA's Expedition 31 spaceship took a Smokey doll with them on their trip to the International Space Station.

Today, Smokey Bear live appearances are more popular than ever, and the Forest Service and State Foresters have many Smokey costumes ready to meet the demand. In addition to schools, Smokey appears at rodeos, sporting events, and parades.

The real-life Smokey is also remembered each year on the anniversary of his rescue from a forest fire in New Mexico. During the first weekend in May, a two-day Smokey Bear Days celebration is held in his hometown of Capitan. There's a parade, concerts, and a log-carving contest. And, of course, kids and adults learn about conservation and fire prevention.

Smokey's popularity has made him an incredibly effective spokesbear for wildfire prevention. Smokey's fire prevention message has helped to reduce the number of fires on America's public lands. In 1944, a year before Smokey made his first appearance, the average number of acres burned by wildfires was 22 million. By 2011, that number had dropped to just 6.6 million. In 2023, 1.5 million acres burned due to human-caused wildfires.

"Entire generations of Americans have grown up with Smokey Bear," said Jim Felton, who started working on the Smokey campaign in the 1940s. "He has become a vital part of American culture. . . . Smokey Bear is a real personality with a real identity to which millions of Americans closely relate. People know and understand Smokey. He is not a stranger. . . . We trust Smokey; he has won our confidence."

In 2001, Smokey's famous message was updated to "Only you can prevent wildfires." The change was made after a large number of wildfires occurred in natural areas other than forests, such as grasslands. In 2022, it was estimated that 87 percent of wildfires were caused by humans.

Smokey has kept his job as America's spokesbear for almost eighty years. A lot of dedicated people have worked hard behind the scenes for all those decades, presenting Smokey and delivering his important messages about wildfire prevention to the public.

Li'l Smokey

During the summer of 2008, more than two thousand wildfires blazed across Northern California. Firefighter Adam Deem found a badly injured bear cub clinging to a tree in one of the burned forests. Adam named the cub Li'l Smokey in honor of the two famous bears, Smokey and Little Smokey, who had both been rescued so many years ago in New Mexico and later lived at the National Zoo.

Instead of traveling to a zoo, though, Li'l Smokey was successfully returned to the wild in Northern California after he recovered from his burns. The Department of Fish and Game attached a small tag to the cub's ear so they could track him. Thanks to that tag, they could tell that Li'l Smokey was alive and well in his new home.

It's likely that Smokey Bear is going to be around for at least another eighty years . . . and probably longer. As long as we have forests and grasslands that need to be protected, we will always need Smokey's most important message: "Remember—Only *You* Can Prevent Wildfires!"

Smokey Online

Smokey has his own Instagram, Facebook, and Twitter accounts. There is also an official Smokey website (www.smokeybear.com/en/smokey-for-kids/about-smokey) where people can learn more about wildfire prevention. The site also has these fun facts about Smokey:

- Smokey is a black bear.

- He weighs over 300 pounds.

- He weighed about one and a half pounds at birth, about as much as a loaf of bread.

- His favorite foods are forest treats such as ants and other insects, salmon and trout, bark, plants, roots, and berries. And honey, too!

- His favorite saying is, "Only you can prevent wildfires."

Bibliography

*Books for young readers

*Bromley, Robin. *The Story of Smokey Bear*. New York: Ladybird Books, 1996.

*Deem, Adam, and Celeste Deem. *Saving Li'l Smokey: A True Story*. Scotts Valley, CA: CreateSpace Independent Publishing Platform, 2009.

Lawter Jr., William Clifford. *Smokey Bear 20252: A Biography*. Alexandria, VA: Lindsay Smith Publishers, 1994.

Morrison, Ellen Earnhardt. *Guardian of the Forest: A History of the Smokey Bear Program*. New York: Vantage Press, Inc., 1976.

*Newman, Paul S. *The True Story of Smokey the Bear*. Racine, WI: Western Publishing Company, Inc., 1960.

Signell, Karen. *Smokey Bear: The Cub Who Left His Pawprints on History*. Boca Raton, FL: Karen Signell, 2014.

*United States Department of Agriculture. *Smokey Bear Story*. Washington, DC: United States Department of Agriculture, 2009.

*Watson, Jane Werner. *The True Story of Smokey the Bear*. New York: Golden Press, 1955.

*Werner, Jane. *Smokey the Bear*. Racine, WI: Western Publishing Company, 1955.